SPECTACULAR SPOOKS

Chosen by Brian Moses

Illustrated by Peter Allen

MACMILLAN CHILDREN'S BOOKS

First published 2000
by Macmillan Children's Books

This edition published 2001
by Macmillan Children's Books
a division of Pan Macmillan Limited
20 New Wharf Road, London N1 9RR
Basingstoke and Oxford
www.panmacmillan.com

Associated companies throughout the world

ISBN 0 330 39206 9

135798642

A CIP catalogue record for this book is available from the British Library

Printed and bound by Mackays of Chatham plc, Kent

Contents

Terrible Toast

"This toast," moaned the ghost
"is impossible to chew.
The trouble is, my teeth
just float right through."

"Allow me," smiled the vampire,
with a grin of delight.
"I'll show you how it's done.
You watch. I'll bite."

So the vampire ate the lot,
but what he liked most
was the red, sticky jam
which he licked from the toast.

Tony Mitton

The Teflon Terror

I know that the monster without a head
Is lying in wait right under my bed,
But being headless, he can't see
What I've brought upstairs with me.
This frying pan should do the trick.

BANG!

(Thank God that monster was non-stick!)

Andrew Fusek Peters

It's Behind You

I don't want to scare you
But just behind you
Is a . . .

No! Don't look!
Just act calmly
As if it wasn't there.

Like I said
Can you hear me if I whisper?
Just behind you
Is a . . .

NO! DON'T LOOK!
Just keep on reading
Don't turn round, believe me
It isn't worth it.

If you could see
What I can see standing there
You'd understand.

It's probably one
Of the harmless sort
Although with that mouth
Not to mention the teeth
And all that blood
Dripping down its chin
I wouldn't like to say.

4

Oh listen
It's trying to speak
I think it wants to be friends.

Oh I see it doesn't, never mind
You'd better leave just in case
I expect you'll escape
If you don't look round.

Oh what a shame!
I thought you'd make it
To the door. Hard luck.
I still think it means no harm
I expect it bites all its friends.

David Harmer

Teasing Ghosts

They are behind me as I walk –
I can hear their whispery talk.
They make the twigs go crack,
and pull faces at my back.

I can feel them stare and stare –
but whenever I turn they're not . . .

Tim Pointon

Where's Sam?

In the night
Quiet and peaceful
Everyone's sleeping
What's that noise?

CLANK! THUMP!
CRASH! BUMP!

Dad, Dad, HELP!

In the night
Quiet and peaceful
Everyone's sleeping
Oh no. It's back!

CLANK! THUMP!
CRASH! BUMP!

Dad, Dad, HELP!

In the night
Quiet and peaceful
Everyone's sleeping
It's after me!

CLANK! THUMP!
CRASH! BUMP!

Dad, Dad, HELP!

In the night
Quiet and peaceful
Everyone's sleeping
It's got me!

CLANK! THUMP!
CRASH! BUMP!

Dad, Dad, HELP!

In the morning
New day dawning
Everyone's waking

but

8

What noise?
I can't hear anything
You imagined it
Go back to sleep

Not again
I can't hear anything
You imagined it
Go back to sleep

Right that's enough
This is ridiculous
You're making it up
Don't call me again

Be quiet, Sam
Stop calling me
I'm not interested

where's Sam?

Andrea Shavick

Who's Afraid?

Do I have to go haunting tonight?
The children might give me a fright.
It's dark in that house.
I might meet a mouse.
Do I have to go haunting tonight?

I don't like the way they scream out,
When they see me skulking about.
I'd rather stay here,
Where there's nothing to fear.
Do I have to go haunting tonight?

John Foster

You Are Invited to a Spook Party

Please come to my party;
Wear something in white.
Tell Mum that you're coming:
It starts at midnight.

Don't bring any jelly;
Don't bring any fizz;
For spooks live on nothing
But air – as it is.

Bring Will-o'-the-wisp;
Bring a glow-worm or two;
And I'll glide on thin air
In a ghost-dance with you.

Mina Johnson

The Skeleton Hop

Rattle your bones. Don't stop.
Then do the skeleton hop.
Chatter your teeth. Click clack
and creak all your joints. Crick crack.
Jangle your ribs right now
then do the skeleton bow.
Rattle those bones. Make a din
and do the skeleton grin.
Right, skeletons, off we go.
Time for the skeleton show.

Marian Swinger

12

Night Creatures

Lizards licking
crickets cricking
bats flapping
snakes slipping
owls scowl
dogs howl
chickens flurry
mongoose hurry
spiders sneaking
frogs creaking
mosquitoes sipping
rats ripping
'GOODNIGHT!'

Pauline Stewart

As I Lay

As I lay
fast awake
last night
something
came to
cause a
fright.

Something
which lives
inside
my head,
but spends
each night
beneath
my bed.

O how
I wish it
would go
away, but
whatever
I do it
seems to
stay.

Lurking
there, where
I dare not
peep; lurking
there until
I fall

a
   s
     l
      e
        e
          p.

Tony Langham

Wilderness Hill

Children never go there
and traffic never slows
on Wilderness Hill.

Winds blow cold there
and stories are told
about Wilderness Hill.

Birds never call there,
avoided by all
is Wilderness Hill.

Now flowers never grow there
but everyone knows
about Wilderness Hill.

Do you?

Brian Moses

Something Horrible

When a full moon, a starry sky
And a dark night
Come together

Something moves in the garden
Something watches
Something waits

When a full moon, a starry sky
And a dark night
Come together

Don't go anywhere near the garden
The Something Horrible
Is awake.

Andrea Shavick

18

Going Upstairs

Only the bravest person dares
To go up the trickety, rickety stairs.

The first step creaks like a bending bone.
On the second there's a stain.
You have to miss the third step out
Or you'll never come down again.

Only the bravest person dares
To go up the trickety, rickety stairs.

Hold your breath on the fourth step.
On the fifth step count to five.
Close your eyes on the sixth step
Or you'll never come down alive.

Only the bravest person dares
To go up the trickety, rickety stairs.

Left foot on the seventh,
On the eighth your right.
Once you reach the ninth step
Your bedroom door's in sight.

Safely on the landing
Keep a steady head:
Cross your fingers as you go
And jump into bed.

Phew!

Celia Warren

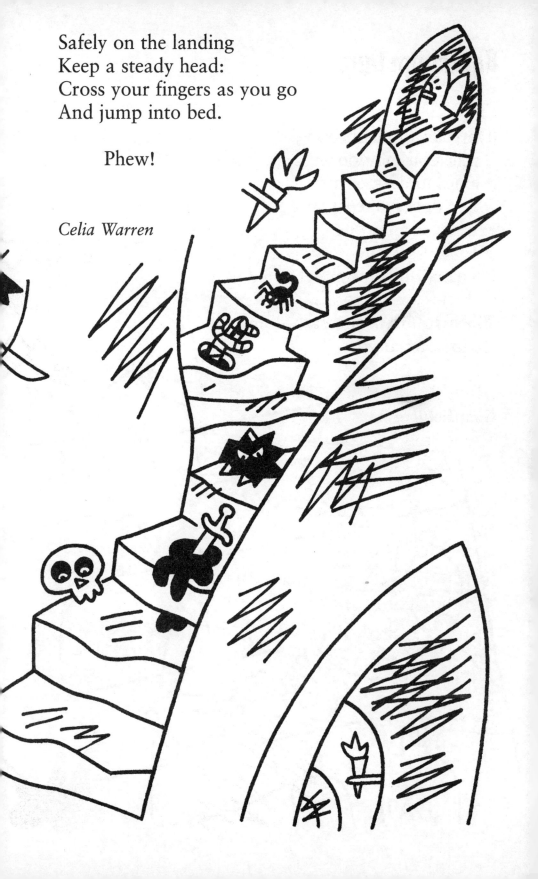

Bathroom Bug

It lives in the bathroom,
it slides on the floor,
it hides in dark corners
where dust makes it snore.

It's hairy and spiky
and sticky with goo.
When you're in the bathroom
it's looking at you.

Gina Douthwaite

The Haunted Rocking Chair

Suddenly, the rocking chair
creaked, though nobody was there.
It rocked, though no one sat in it.
The room was cosy, fire lit,
with children eating buttered toast,
and, in the rocking chair, a ghost.
Though no one saw it, it was there,
rocking in the rocking chair.

Marian Swinger

How Scary!

I'm frightened of my shadow
And I'm frightened of the dark;
I'm frightened, too, of next-door's dog,
Or of being eaten by a shark;
But what gets REALLY spooky,
As I'm sure you will agree,
Is when I give a little burp –
And the teacher KNOWS it's ME!

Trevor Harvey

Who's Counting?

One for a shadow
Two for a scare
Three for a cobweb
    in my hair.

Four for a whisper
Five for a scream
Six for a monster
    in my dream.

Seven for a shiver
up my spine:
Reach for the light switch –
    just in time!

Celia Warren

Spooky House

Listen, hear the creak
  of the old floorboard.
Look, see the gleam
  of the sharp-edged sword.
Sniff, smell the dust
  in the stale, damp air.
Touch, feel the cobwebs
  hanging down the dark stair.

Do I hear a ghost
  tapping on the windowpane?
No, it's just my brother's
  teeth chattering again!

Penny Kent

It's Dark!

It's dark
and my curtains are
  e a p
l   i n g
across my room.

It's dark
and my toys are
peeping
from under my bed.

It's dark
and my clothes are
cr   eep   ing
over my sofa.

It's dark
and shadows are
s   i n g
  w   p
    e e
across my carpet.

It's dark
and . . .
I . . .
should . . .
be . . . (yawn)
ZZZZzzzzleeping!

Ian Souter

My Little Monster

I keep a little monster at the bottom of my bed.
Before I go to sleep at night he pats me on the
    head.

My room is always in a mess (it makes my
    parents shout),
because my little monster likes to throw my toys
    about.

He spills my drink at breakfast and he loses shoes
    as well,
because he knows that no one will believe me if I
    tell.

One day he tore the curtains. "It's my monster,
    Mum," I said.
My monster got away scot-free, and I got sent to
    bed.

I take my little monster every day with me to
    school.
One day he made rude noises very loudly in the
    hall.

It doesn't matter what I say. It turns out just the
    same –
my monster simply disappears and I'm the one
    they blame.

Charles Thomson

Have You Ever?

Have you ever . . .
been on a ghost train,
where bats fly,
the shadows sigh
and darkness moans?

Have you ever . . .
heard on a ghost train,
click-clack wheels,
the skeleton squeals
and rattling bones?

Have you ever . . .
seen on a ghost train,
spiders dangle,
cobwebs tangle,
grey tombstones?

Have you ever . . .
felt on a ghost train . . .

NO THANKS!

Judith Nicholls

Advice to a Young Ghost

"Please remember,

Whatever you do,

Don't spook until

You're spooken to."

Trevor Harvey

You Don't Frighten Me!

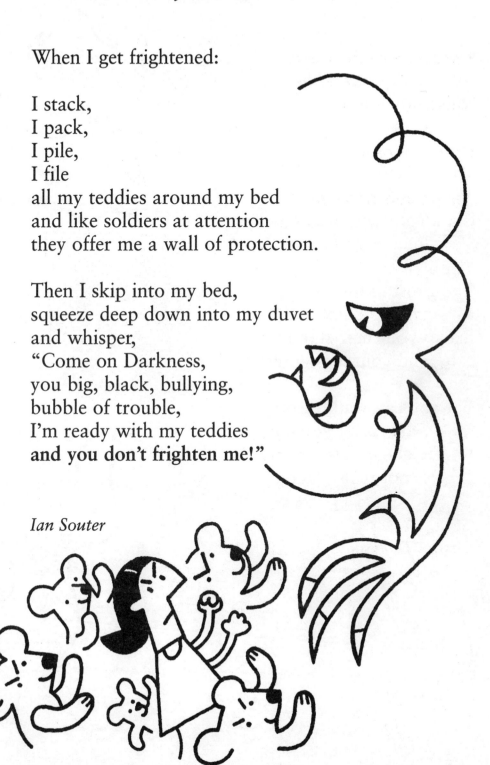

When I get frightened:

I stack,
I pack,
I pile,
I file
all my teddies around my bed
and like soldiers at attention
they offer me a wall of protection.

Then I skip into my bed,
squeeze deep down into my duvet
and whisper,
"Come on Darkness,
you big, black, bullying,
bubble of trouble,
I'm ready with my teddies
and you don't frighten me!"

Ian Souter

The Ghost in the Castle

The ghost in the castle
    tu-whit tu-whoo
walks down the stairs.
      He's looking at you.

The ghost in the castle
    clank clank rattle
is a knight who was killed
      long ago in battle.

The ghost in the castle
    tap tap creak
makes your hair stand on end
      and your legs go weak.

But you can walk through him
    (you can if you dare)
for the ghost in the castle
      is not really there.

Charles Thomson

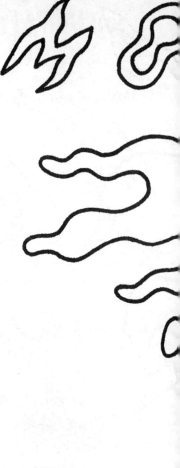
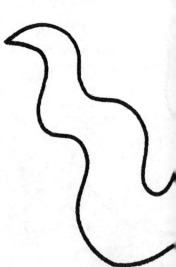

Who's There?

Nobody breaks the windows,
Nobody spills the milk.
Nobody creeps round the house at night
As silent and secret as smooth black silk.

Nobody digs deep holes in the garden,
Nobody scratches long scars in the wall.
I am afraid of Nobody.
When I'm alone will Nobody call?

Nobody whispers scary stories
To frighten the little ones tucked in their beds.
Nobody growls and makes wicked noises
To make them pull covers over their heads.

When there's just me by myself, I will shudder.
Hush myself. Still myself. Shiver with fear,
Because, in the shadows, I know who is waiting –
Watchful and hungry – Nobody's here . . .

Jan Dean

A Few Bathroom Beasts

I'm the gurgly giant behind the sink:
When you turn on the tap
For a midnight drink
The bathroom mirror will give you a wink
And when I'm in the mood to tease
I'll reach through the tiles and tickle your knees.

I'm the spider lurking down the plug.
With hairy legs and an ugly mug
And a gob full of teeth
Set out in rows;
When you're in the bath,
I'll bite your toes!

David Orme

Not Scared

Who is it?
Where is it?
How is it?
Why?

I'm not scared
And I won't cry.

I'll lie here alone
In my own brave bed,
And friendly dreams
Will soon fill my head.

John Kitching

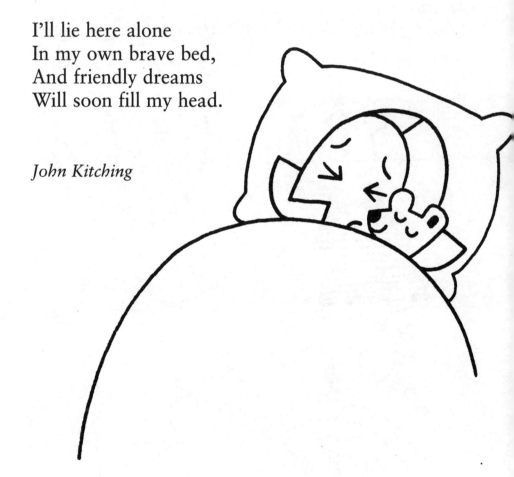

Is It True?

"You don't believe in phantoms?
You don't believe I'm true?
That's fine by me,"
Said the little ghost.
"I don't believe in YOU!"

Clare Bevan

The Caretaker

At Gloomy Street School, at end of day,
When the children go,
When the shadows grow,
The ghost of the Caretaker comes to play.

He picks up his broom with a happy sigh,
And he sweeps the floors
And he walks through doors,
As the dust swirls round in the moonlit sky.

At Gloomy Street School at break of day,
While the classrooms gleam,
While the teachers dream,
The ghost of the Caretaker creeps away.

Clare Bevan

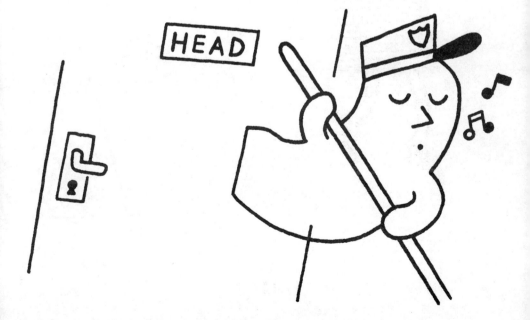

Do You Want to Be a Wizard?

Do you want to be a wizard?
  Well, you'll need a pointed hat
  with silver stars and golden moon,
  and perched on top . . . a bat.

Do you want to be a wizard?
  Well, you'll need *Ye Booke of Spells*
  and rotten eggs and fried frogs' legs
  to make some horrid smells.

Do you want to be a wizard?
  Well, you'll need some pickled brains,
  a wand, a cloak, and one dead rat,
  and green slime from the drains.

Do you *still* want to be a wizard?

Wes Magee

All Alone

I'm a lonely ghost,
A lonely ghost.
Nobody plays with me.
I'm sad and miserable,
Empty and low.
Nobody knows how I feel.

My thin heart aches
For a friendly word,
A laugh, a joke, a smile
    – so
I pluck up the courage
To show myself
And folk scream
    – they run a mile!

Is it any wonder
I'm wrapped in grey?
That I'm chilled
To my ghostly bones?
Is it any wonder
I sigh in the night?
Is it any wonder
I moan?

Patricia Leighton

Ghoul School Rules

1. Glide, don't flit!

2. Keep your head ON at all times.

3. NO clanking of chains between lessons.

4. No walking through walls. Wait OUTSIDE the classroom.

5. No skeletons to be taken out of cupboards.

6. Line up QUIETLY for the ghost train at the end of the night.

Sue Cowling

Witches United

Warty-nose Wanda
Pointy-hat Pru
Black-cat Camilla
And Hairy-toes Lou
Broomstick Morwena
Skinny-legs Gertie
The last place goes
To "Dingwall the Dirty".

They're ugly, they're smelly
They're nasty and mean
They're the "Witches United"
Netball team.

Richard Caley

Things Which Go Bump

There's a ghost in our cupboard
a monster behind the door,
a large green dragon peering
through a crack in the floor.

A pair of giant bats
flapping round my bed,
a fierce dinosaur,
its eyes flashing red.

A creature standing still
in the middle of the night,
so where do they all go
when I turn on the light?

Andrew Collett

Midnight

.1/43 .42

.2 .41

.3 .40

.4 .39

.5 .38

.6 .37

.15 .28

.7

She saw something
in a snow-white dress.
"Are you a g-g-g-ghost?"

"Yes."

.36

.8 .14 .29 .35

.10 .12 .31 .33

.9 .11 .13 .30 .32 .34

.16 .20 .21 .22 .23 .27

.17 .26

.18 .19 .24 .25

Mike Johnson

Who'd be a Ghost?

"I won't go!" said young Fred
as his mum
dusted him up
to go haunting.
                "*You will!*"
                his mum said.
"But I hate it there," said Fred.
                "*Untidy your hair,*"
                she said.

"Can't I haunt
somewhere else?"
begged Fred.
                "*Don't be a wimp!*"
                she said.
"A castle – a barn – a flat?
A black and white pub?"
                "*Uncle Harold's got that.*"

"Mum – mum, I feel sick."
                "*No, you don't,*"
                she said:
                "*Now for goodness sake,
                you'll be late!
                Stop moaning,
                start groaning
                and GO!*"

"This is the last time!
The *very last time*!" muttered Fred
as he hovered
at the edge
of the M6 motorway.
"A ghost could
end up DEAD
doing this!"

Patricia Leighton

Noises in the Night

What's that scratching
at the window-pane?
Who's that knocking
again and again?
What's that creeping
across the floor?
And who's that tapping
at my bedroom door?

What's that creaking
beneath my bed?
Who's that walking
with a slow slow tread?
What's that whirring
in the air?
And who's that coming
up the squeaky stair?

I lie in bed
and I'm wide awake.
The noises make me
shiver and shake.
But soon all's quiet
and the dark is deep
so I close my eyes
and fall a . . .

Wes Magee

Gobbledespook

Can you read this message?
The bottom of each letter
was bitten off and gobbled
by a ghost who knew no better

Gina Douthwaite